BULFINCH'S MYTHOLOGY
Coloring Book

BULFINCH'S MYTHOLOGY
Coloring Book

Retold by Steven Zorn

R U N N I N G   P R E S S
Philadelphia, Pennsylvania

Canadian representatives: General Publishing Co., Ltd., 30 Lesmill Road, Don Mills, Ontario M3B 2T6

International representatives: Worldwide Media Services, Inc., 115 East Twenty-third Street, New York, NY 10010.

9 8 7 6 5 4 3 2

Digit on the right indicates the number of this printing.

ISBN 0-89471-710-3

Cover design by Toby Schmidt
Cover illustrations by Helen I. Driggs
Interior illustrations by Helen I. Driggs
Printed by Chernay Printing, Inc., Coopersburg, Pennsylvania.
Typography by Commcor Communications Corporation, Philadelphia, Pennsylvania
This book may be ordered by mail from the publisher.
Please add $2.50 for postage and handling.
But try your bookstore first!
Running Press Book Publishers
125 South Twenty-second Street
Philadelphia, Pennsylvania 19103

Introduction

The world is full of mystery: Seasons change, plants grow, babies are born, couples fall in love, and nations go to war against each other.

To find answers to life's mysteries, the ancient Greeks and Romans invented gods and goddesses. Everything that humans saw or experienced was explained by the whims or plans of these immortal beings.

But the gods and goddesses were not perfect. They were often vain and short-tempered, sometimes deceitful, and not always fair with one another. They lived on the summit of Mount Olympus in northeastern Greece, where they controlled the destiny of mortals and quarrelled among themselves. They could change into any creature, but they usually took human forms.

The 16 stories in this book offer a glimpse of the classic tales of gods and mortals, power and faith, and tolerance and foolishness that have been retold for thousands of years. Although the Greeks and the Romans worshipped the same gods, they called them by different names. The names in this book are Roman.

Jupiter was the king of the gods, and he ruled over the gods and mortals. When he walked, he made thunder. His scepter was a lightning bolt, with which he would strike the earth when angered. Jupiter's wife was Juno. Juno and Jupiter loved each other, but Jupiter also enjoyed courting other women, both divine and mortal. His schemes to prevent his jealous wife from discovering his cheating form the heart of many of the great myths.

The Greeks and Romans saw that life was much too complicated to be controlled by only Juno and Jupiter. They created other gods, each with a distinct job, to take part in the affairs of everyday life.

Apollo was the god of archery, prophecy, music, and the sun. His sister, Diana, was goddess of the moon and of the hunt.

Venus was the goddess of love and beauty. Her son was Cupid, the god of love, who was armed with darts of desire.

Minerva was the goddess of wisdom, who sprang from Jupiter's head and had no mother.

Mercury was the god of commerce, gymnastics, and any skill that required dexterity—including theft.

Pluto was the ruler of the land of the dead; Neptune ruled the sea; and Mars was the god of war.

Nine sister goddesses, called Muses, inspired mortals to create literature, art, and science.

Grotesque monsters in all shapes roamed the unexplored parts of the earth, but there were also nymphs, the peaceable daughters of the gods who inhabited forests, streams, and meadows. Over the years, the nymphs have become the storybook spirits who we call fairies.

The tales in this book have been adapted from *The Age of Fable* by Thomas Bulfinch. Thomas was the son of Charles Bulfinch, the architect of the Capitol Building in Washington, D.C. He was born in Boston, where he taught Latin for a year, and then worked as a bank clerk.

Passionate about the myths of the ancients, Bulfinch wrote *The Age of Fable* in 1855, hoping to make these wonderful stories accessible to modern readers. He later wrote *The Age of Chivalry* and *Legends of Charlemagne*, which retold the tales of medieval times. To this day, Bulfinch's works remain the most highly regarded books of myths and legends.

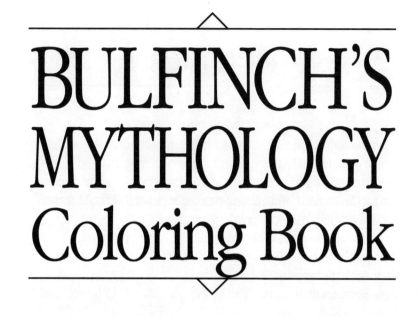

BULFINCH'S MYTHOLOGY
Coloring Book

Hercules

Jupiter, king of the gods, had several mortal children. His most famous child was Hercules, the strongest man on earth.

Jupiter's wife, Juno, queen of the gods, was hostile toward her husband's human children. She especially disliked Hercules, who, though mortal, had the strength of a god.

When Hercules was a few weeks old, Juno sent two snakes to destroy him as he lay in his cradle. The baby Hercules strangled them with his bare hands.

As Hercules grew to manhood, Juno continued testing him, and Hercules always passed the tests. This enraged Juno. Finally, she ordered Hercules to perform a series of dangerous tasks, which became known as the Twelve Labors of Hercules. Jupiter, confident that his son could pass these tests, and feeling that Hercules would be an inspiration to other mortals, allowed Juno to order Hercules to perform the labors.

Hercules	HUR-kyoo-leez
Nemean Lion	NEE-mee-un
Augeas	uh-JEE-us
Hyppolyta	hih-PAHL-uh-tuh
Hesperides	hess-PER-uh-deez

Most of the labors involved killing ferocious animals, like the Nemean Lion and the Hydra.

The Nemean Lion was a beast that terrorized the valley of Nemea. Clubs and arrows were useless against it, so Hercules used his childhood trick and choked it to death.

The Hydra was a monster with nine heads. The middle head was immortal, and when any of the monster's other eight heads were cut off, two would grow back.

As Hercules chopped off each head, he burned the wound with a flaming torch, preventing new growth. Then he buried the immortal head under a boulder.

Hercules' next job was much less dangerous, but much dirtier. A king named Augeas had a herd of 3,000 oxen whose stalls had not been cleaned for 30 years. Hercules was ordered to thoroughly clean each stable, a task that could take years to finish. It was a humiliating assignment, hardly fit for a hero, but Hercules handled it in truly heroic fashion. Rather than shoveling the dirt, Hercules changed the courses of two nearby rivers to run through the stables and wash away the filth. He finished the cleaning job in a single day.

Hercules' next labor was more delicate. He was ordered to obtain the queen of the Amazons' belt.

The Amazons were a warlike nation of women. Hercules went to the Amazons and was warmly welcomed by Hippolyta, their queen. Amused that Hercules had come for her belt, she presented it to him as a gift.

Juno, angry that this labor had gone so smoothly, took the form of an Amazon and persuaded the others that Hercules was carrying off Hippolyta.

The Amazons attacked Hercules' crew. Hercules, thinking that Hippolyta had betrayed him, slew her.

Hercules' most difficult labor was gathering the golden apples of the Hesperides.

The apples had been given to Juno as a wedding present from the goddess of the earth. They were guarded by three sisters known as the Hesperides.

The Hesperides were the daughters of Atlas, a giant from a race older than the gods, called the Titans. Long ago, the Titans and the gods fought. The gods won and punished the Titans. Atlas was punished by having to bear the weight of the earth on his shoulders forever.

Hercules didn't know where to find the Hesperides, so he asked Atlas to get the apples for him. Atlas was eager to be relieved of his burden for a while, and Hercules was the only person strong enough for the job of holding the earth.

One by one, Hercules successfully completed each of his twelve tasks. Finally, he won the friendship of Juno and was granted immortality.

The Riddle of the Sphinx

A prince named Oedipus was traveling through the Greek countryside when he neared the city of Thebes. The road to the city was blocked by a monster called the Sphinx. She had the body of a lion and the head and torso of a woman. She lay crouched on top of a rock, stopping all travelers to ask them a riddle.

Any traveler who solved the riddle could pass; but those who failed were killed.

When Oedipus approached the Sphinx, no one had yet solved the puzzle. The city had become a prison; its citizens were afraid to leave, and no one could enter.

But Oedipus was ready for the challenge. The Sphinx was happy to find another victim.

"What animal," asked the Sphinx, "walks in the morning on four feet, in the afternoon on two feet, and in the evening on three feet?"

Oedipus   ED-uh-pus
Thebes   theebz

Oedipus thought a moment. Then he replied, "The answer is Man.

"In childhood he creeps on hands and knees, in manhood he walks upright, and in old age he walks with the aid of a cane."

The Sphinx was so outraged that Oedipus solved her riddle that she threw herself off the rock to her death.

The people of Thebes showed their thanks to Oedipus by making him king.

The Face that Launched a Thousand Ships

Minerva was the goddess of wisdom, but one day she did a very foolish thing: she entered into a beauty competition with Juno, the queen of the gods, and Venus, the goddess of love.

Here's how it happened:

It was the occasion of the most festive wedding ever witnessed—even by the gods. The bride was Thetis, a beautiful sea nymph. Her bridegroom was King Peleus, a mighty—but mortal— warrior. All the gods were invited to this spectacular affair. All, that is, except Eris, the goddess of discord.

Would Eris stand for such a slight? Absolutely not! Creating conflict was a game to her; disruption was her talent. She couldn't let such an opportunity pass.

The most dangerous plans are also the most simple, and nothing could surpass the simplicity of Eris's evil scheme. During the wedding feast, she sneaked invisibly into the banquet room and rolled a single golden apple down the banquet table. On the apple was inscribed "To the Fairest."

Minerva	mih-NUR-vuh
Thetis	THEE-tis
Peleus	PEE-lee-us
Eris	EE-ris
Menelaus	men-ih-LAY-us

23

The apple stopped right in front of Minerva, Juno, and Venus. The three beautiful and usually dignified goddesses were also very vain. Together, they lunged after the apple, each one claiming to be its rightful owner. They asked Jupiter, king of all the gods, to choose the fairest, but he was too wise to make such a delicate decision. He suggested that the goddesses pay a visit to young Paris, the prince of Troy, who was a lover of beauty. The goddesses agreed.

Paris was working as a shepherd because his father, the king of Troy, had been warned that his son would bring about the downfall of the kingdom, and so sent him away. The three goddesses appeared before a very startled Paris as he tended his flock, and asked him to decide who should have the apple.

As Paris gazed at the three goddesses, considering his answer, each leaned forward and whispered in his ear, hoping to influence his decision. Juno promised him power and riches. Minerva promised glory and renown in war. Venus promised him the fairest mortal woman for his wife: Queen Helen of Sparta. Paris awarded the apple, which became known as the Apple of Discord, to Venus.

Every eligible man in Greece had sought Helen's hand, but King Menelaus of Sparta had won her. Out of honor, all the other Greek men swore to always protect Helen from harm. Paris, protected by Venus, sailed to Sparta. King Menelaus welcomed him into his home, never suspecting Paris to kidnap his wife.

Upon the discovery of this treacherous act, the Greek army sent 1,000 warships to Troy to reclaim the Spartan queen. It was the beginning of the Trojan War, a 10-year battle between the world's fiercest armies. Even the gods took sides.

Beware of Greeks Bearing Gifts

The war between Troy and Greece raged 10 years, but it would have lasted longer if not for the crafty Greeks.

In Troy there was a famous statue of Minerva, goddess of wisdom, called the Palladium. It was said to have fallen from heaven. Everyone believed that the city could not be defeated as long as the statue remained within it.

Ulysses and Diomed, two of the great war heroes on the Greek side, disguised themselves, sneaked into the walled city of Troy, and stole the statue. Then the Greek army attacked the city of Troy once again.

Minerva	mih-NUR-vuh
Palladium	puh-LAY-dee-um
Ulysses	yu-LISS-eez
Diomed	DY-o-meed
Laocoön	lay-AHK-oh-un

But Troy still held out, and the Greeks began to fear they could never win it by force. Something more clever was called for, and Ulysses was the one to think of it.

The Greek army pretended to abandon the battle. Most of the troops were withdrawn, and the warships were hidden behind a nearby island. The remaining men built an enormous wooden horse before sailing away.

The Trojans saw that the Greeks were gone and assumed they had given up. The gates of Troy were thrown open and the citizens flooded out, rejoicing at their freedom.

The sight of the empty Greek camp was surprising. Even more astonishing was that great horse. What could it be for? Some suggested taking it into the city as a trophy. Others were afraid of it—and wisely so, because within the belly of the horse hid some of Greece's fiercest warriors.

While the Trojans were considering what to do with this strange souvenir, Laocoön, the priest of the sea god Neptune, exclaimed, "Citizens, what madness is this? Have you not learned enough of the Greeks to be on your guard against them?

"I fear the Greeks even when they offer gifts."

Laocoön threw his spear against the massive horse, and the statue rang hollow. The Trojans' suspicion was aroused, but only for a moment, because just then some scouts returned, dragging a Greek prisoner.

The captive was brought before the Trojan chiefs, who promised to spare his life if he answered their questions truly.

The sobbing prisoner said his name was Sinon and that he was a soldier in the Greek army under Ulysses' command. Sinon told the Trojans that Ulysses thought he was a coward and had left him behind to die.

But Sinon was far from being a coward. He was a brave Greek warrior, and the story he told was made up by Ulysses to win the Trojans' trust.

Sinon told the Trojans that the Greeks felt they had offended Minerva by stealing the Palladium. The horse was built as a gift to Minerva in hopes of winning back her favor, he explained.

Sinon, a skillful and convincing teller of tales, was crying uncontrollably as he went on: The horse was built huge to prevent it from being carried within the walls of Troy. A prophet had told Ulysses that if the Trojans took it, they would surely win the war, he said.

Most of the citizens were thrilled by this news. Those who still doubted were convinced by what happened next.

The sea god Neptune favored the Greeks over the Trojans. To make Sinon's story even more believable, he sent two enormous sea serpents to devour Laocoön and his two sons as the horrified crowd looked on. This was seen as proof that the gods were angered by Laocoön's disrespectful treatment of the sacred horse.

Triumphant, the Trojans brought the horse into their city amid songs and celebrations.

Later that night, while the people of Troy lay sleeping, overcome by their feast and festivities, Sinon released the horse's deadly cargo. The troops within the horse opened the gates of the city to the rest of the Greek army, which had returned under cover of darkness.

Troy fell that night, and a long and bloody war was ended.

Ulysses

In their haste to return home after winning the Trojan War, the Greeks forgot to thank the gods for their victory. So the gods turned against them.

To punish Ulysses, king of Ithaca and hero of the Trojan War, the gods created one misadventure after another, delaying his return to his family.

One of the first obstacles Ulysses and his crew faced was the Lotus-eaters. This kindly race entertained the men on their island and served them the seeds of the delicate water plant. Those who ate the lotus lost all memory of home and wished to remain on the island. Ulysses was forced to drag his crew away from their hosts and tie each man to the ship so that they could sail.

Ulysses	yu-LISS-eez	**Circe**	SIR-see
Ithaca	ITH-uh-kuh	**Charybdis**	kuh-RIB-dis
Cyclopes	sy-KLO-peez	**Scylla**	SIL-uh
Cyclops	SY-klops	**Penelope**	pe-NEL-uh-pee
Polyphemus	pahl-ih-FEE-mus	**Telemachus**	te-LEM-uh-kis
Aeaea	EE-EE-uh		

Next they arrived in the country of the Cyclopes. Each of these fearsome giants had a single eye in the middle of his forehead. Ulysses' ships landed on the island to gather supplies, but one Cyclops, Polyphemus, imprisoned the crew and began to devour them two at a time. Ulysses managed to blind the Cyclops and escape with the survivors.

Polyphemus was the son of the powerful sea god Neptune. Furious that Ulysses had wounded his son, Neptune did all he could to prevent Ulysses from reaching home.

Everywhere the ships landed, danger awaited. On the beautiful isle of Aeaea, the crew was met by lions, wolves, and tigers. The men were surprised to discover that the beasts were all tame as puppies. The real danger was a powerful magician named Circe, who had put the wild animals under a spell. Circe seemed to be a gracious host. She prepared tempting meals for the men, sang to them, made certain they were comfortable—and then she turned them into pigs!

Mercury, the messenger god, helped Ulysses rescue his men. After that, Circe promised no more tricks, and warned Ulysses of the dangers that awaited once he left the island.

Among these dangers were the Sirens, creatures with the bodies of birds and the faces of beautiful women. They lived on a rocky coast and sang a song irresistible to any man. Sailors hearing their melody would dive into the sea and drown.

Circe told Ulysses to put wax in his crew's ears and have them tie him to the mast so that he could hear, but be unable to obey, the songs of death.

The sea was calm as the sailors approached the Sirens' island. Over the glassy waters came notes so attractive that tears streamed down Ulysses' face as he struggled to get loose. He begged his men to release him, but they only tied him tighter. They held the ship on course and the music grew fainter until Ulysses could not hear it at all. At last he stopped struggling and, with a nod of his head, Ulysses gave his companions the signal to unseal their ears and untie him.

There were still other hazards. The only route home was through a narrow passage between a great whirlpool called Charybdis and a huge, six-headed snake known as Scylla.

Ulysses kept strict watch as the ship approached these two perils. The roar of the waters warned that the ship was nearing Charybdis, but Scylla could not be seen. As Ulysses and his men anxiously watched for the dreaded whirlpool, Scylla darted forth her snaky heads and carried six shrieking crewmen to her den.

Deeply saddened by the loss of their friends, the men sailed on and faced other dangers. Only Ulysses survived all the hardships placed before him by the gods.

At last Ulysses reached Ithaca, where he was reunited with his wife, Penelope, and his son, Telemachus, who was born just before the war began. Ulysses proved that one person's determination can be stronger than the anger of all the gods.

Penelope

Ulysses married Penelope, a lovely, intelligent woman, less than a year before the Trojan War began. Together they had a son, Telemachus. When Telemachus was just a few weeks old, his father went away to war.

The Trojan War kept Ulysses from his family for 10 years. Because the gods were angry with him, his return to Ithaca took another 10 years.

When the war ended, Penelope waited patiently in Ithaca for Ulysses. Several years after the war ended, Penelope began to be hounded by men who wanted to marry her.

"The war has been over a great while," one of the men said. "If Ulysses is not home by now, he is most certainly dead."

Some of the suitors were officers who had returned from the Trojan War. Others were noblemen from neighboring kingdoms who, by marrying Penelope, could take over Ulysses' kingdom and expand their own land.

These uninvited, unwelcome guests moved into Penelope's home, slaughtered and ate her cattle and sheep, and refused to leave until Penelope chose a new husband. They treated Telemachus like a servant and even threatened to carry Penelope off if she did not choose a husband soon.

Penelope's faith in Ulysses never wavered. She knew that her husband would one day return to reclaim his kingdom. She did what she could to avoid being forced into remarriage.

Penelope	pe-NEL-uh-pee
Ulysses	yu-LISS-eez
Telemachus	te-LEM-uh-kis
Ithaca	ITH-uh-kuh

She remained friendly to the suitors, letting them think that she was considering marrying one of them. This tactic worked for a long time, but then the men grew impatient and demanded an answer.

Penelope created a clever plan. She told the suitors that she would remarry, but only after she finished knitting an elaborate burial cloth for Ulysses' father, now a very old man. Though the suitors were brutes, they could not deny Penelope this sacred task.

By day, Penelope wove together the threads of the exquisite cloth, but each night she would secretly unravel it by torchlight. She kept this up for more than three years before the suitors discovered her trick.

Meanwhile, Ulysses struggled mightily against the gods to return home. Just as Penelope was beginning to lose hope, Ulysses reached Ithaca. With the help of Telemachus, now a young man, Ulysses rid his house of the suitors and was reunited with his wife.

Daedalus and Icarus

On the Isle of Crete lived a brutal monster called the Minotaur. It had a bull's muscular body, a grotesque, barely human face, horns, and sharp teeth. It was extremely strong and fierce.

Minos, the king of Crete, kept the Minotaur in a maze built by Daedalus, a master craftsman. The Minotaur's maze was artfully designed. With its numberless winding passages, twists, and turns, it seemed to have neither beginning nor end.

Minos was a cruel ruler. He ordered that each year seven young men and seven young women be sent to their deaths by being locked in the maze. There the Minotaur roamed, waiting for its next meal of human flesh.

The friendship of an evil king is not to be trusted. Soon after building the maze, Daedalus lost the king's favor. He and his young son Icarus were condemned to live in the maze until the Minotaur found and devoured them.

So perfect was the maze that even its builder could not escape from its tangled halls. Still, Daedalus planned his escape. He knew he could not leave the island by sea because Minos searched every ship.

"Minos may control the land and sea," said Daedalus, "but not the air. I will try that way."

Daedalus	DED-uh-lus
Icarus	IK-uh-rus
Minos	MY-nos
Minotaur	MIN-o-tor
Aegean Sea	ih-JEE-in

Daedalus gathered feathers which he fastened together with bits of string and globs of wax. Young Icarus would chase after the feathers that blew away, or he would sit by his father and play with the wax.

Before long, Daedalus had completed two sets of wings. He strapped one set to himself and, flapping them gently, began to rise gracefully. With a little practice, Daedalus was able to fly forward and backward, and to suspend himself in air. Next, he fitted Icarus with the other pair of wings and taught the excited boy to master them.

When the two were ready to fly beyond the walls of their prison, Daedalus spoke with a trembling voice:

"Icarus, my son, you must remember not to fly too high, for the heat of the sun can melt your wings. Keep near me and you will be safe."

Daedalus rose slowly into the air, and Icarus followed behind. Occasionally the father would glance back to see his boy's progress. As they flew, the plowman stopped his work to gaze and the shepherd leaned on his staff to watch them, astonished at the sight and thinking them to be gods.

Thrilled by the feeling of freedom, Icarus forgot his father's words and began to soar upward as if to reach heaven. The blazing sun softened the wax which held the feathers together. One by one they began to drop away. Icarus wildly waved his arms, but no feathers remained to pin him to the air.

"Father!" he cried, as he plunged into the sea.

"Icarus, Icarus, where are you?" his father shouted. At last he looked down and saw the remains of his child's wings floating on the Aegean Sea.

In his son's memory, Daedalus named the spot the Icarian Sea. It has been called that ever since.

Poor King Midas

King Midas was a fair ruler, but his words always got him into trouble.

Bacchus, the god of wine, learned his craft from a jolly old deity named Silenus. Once, Silenus wandered into Midas's country, where the king played host to him for a few days before returning him to Bacchus. Bacchus, overjoyed that no harm had come to his master, offered Midas whatever he might wish. The king didn't pause to think before replying: "I wish for all I touch to be turned to gold."

Bacchus agreed, but he was sorry that Midas had not made a better choice.

Midas hastened to put his new power to the test. He plucked a branch from an oak and it turned to gold. He picked up a rock, and it too became gold.

It was true! The king could scarcely believe his good fortune.

After several hours of gold-making, the king worked up quite an appetite. He went home to a splendid meal. At first he was amused when he reached for the bread and it turned to gold. But when the same thing happened to his wine, then to his salad, and then to his meat, Midas was horrified.

His wish had become a curse; starvation seemed to await him. He hated his gift and prayed for Bacchus to remove it. Bacchus heard him and consented.

"Go," said Bacchus, "to the River Pactolus. Plunge in and wash away your power."

Midas jumped into the river and his gold-making ability passed into the waters. Even today, gold may be found among the sands of that river.

Midas   MY-dus
Bacchus   BAK-us

After such a terrible experience, Midas rejected wealth and moved to the country to live a simple life. There he worshipped Pan, the bearded, cloven-hoofed god of the fields who played wonderful tunes on reed pipes.

One day, Pan challenged the mighty Apollo, god of the sun and also god of music, to a musical competition. Midas was one of the judges.

Pan blew his reeds beautifully; Apollo chose the lyre, and his skill was superb. Everyone but Midas agreed that Apollo's music was sweeter. Midas protested that the judges favored Apollo not for his skill but because he was the more powerful of the two gods.

Apollo, enraged that Midas would question his talent, bellowed that Midas's hearing was coarse and untrained. To prove his point, Apollo turned the king's ears into those of a mule.

The king's long hair hid his shame from all but his barber, who was sworn to secrecy. But such a juicy secret is hard to keep. Frustrated, the barber went to a meadow, dug a deep hole, whispered the story into it, and covered the hole.

Before long, a thick patch of reeds sprung up at that spot. Whenever the wind blew, the reeds could be heard to whisper "the king has mule's ears . . . the king has mule's ears . . . ."

Orpheus and Eurydice

Can love conquer death? Orpheus believed so.

Orpheus was the son of the sun god Apollo and the goddess Calliope, who inspired mortals to write poetry. His father gave him a stringed instrument called a lyre and taught him to play it. Orpheus played with such perfection that wild beasts would peacefully gather around him, trees would pull up their roots and follow him, and even rocks would soften to the strains of his instrument and the tender words he sang.

The love of Orpheus's life was a woman named Eurydice. The two were married only a short time when tragedy struck.

One day, as Eurydice wandered through a field, a shepherd became entranced by her charm and began to chase her. Fleeing from him, Eurydice stepped on a snake. The snake bit her on the foot, and she died.

Orpheus could not contain his grief over the loss of his bride. He sang prayers to the gods and poured out his sorrow to his friends, but nothing eased his sadness.

At last he decided to visit Tartarus, the land of the dead, and make a personal plea to Pluto, lord of the underworld, for the return of his wife.

Orpheus	OR-fee-us	**Charon**	KAR-un
Calliope	kuh-LY-o-pee	**Cerberus**	SIR-bur-is
Eurydice	yu-RID-ih-see	**Proserpine**	PRAHS-ur-pyn
Chimeras	kuh-MEER-uhz	**Sisyphus**	SIS-uh-fuss

Tartarus was a kingdom of horrors. Those who had committed crimes during their lifetimes paid for those crimes forever. Terrifying monsters made certain that all who entered could never escape.

The passage to Tartarus was through a cave filled with the demons Grief, Worry, Disease, Age, Fear, Hunger, Toil, Poverty, and Death, in forms too dreadful to view. Fire-breathing Chimeras, and nine-headed, hissing Hydras lurked in the darkness. Also there were the Furies, hideous sister goddesses who tormented anyone who had committed a crime that had not been discovered.

Beyond this passage, more horrors awaited. But Orpheus would not turn back. All the demons of Tartarus could not equal the pain of life without Eurydice.

Orpheus came to the bank of a black river where thousands of passengers waited anxiously to be ferried across. Charon, the ferryman, chose only those who had received a proper burial.

"While you still live, you cannot be my passenger," spoke Charon, in a voice chilling to hear.

"I come to seek my wife, whom you brought across this dark, sad river only a short time ago. Please let me find her," Orpheus pleaded. He then sang a song of Eurydice, comparing the depths of his love for her to the bottomless depths of Charon's river.

The song won Charon's sympathy. He allowed Orpheus to board his craft. It groaned under the weight of its live passenger.

At last he was in Tartarus, which was guarded by Cerberus, a ferocious, three-headed dog. Orpheus sang the dog to sleep and entered the gate.

First he heard the wailing of children and of people who had been wrongly executed. Then he passed into the region of sadness, where heartbroken lovers were not freed from pain even by death.

Orpheus found himself before the thrones of Pluto and Proserpine, the king and queen of Tartarus.

"What mortal dares to visit the haunts of the dead while he himself still breathes?" demanded Pluto.

"Oh gods of the underworld," sang Orpheus, as he played his lyre, "hear my words, for they are true. I do not wish to learn your secrets, nor to defy you. I come to seek my wife, whose years were ended by a viper's fang.

"Love has led me here," Orpheus sang, "Love, a god all-powerful with us who live on earth, and who is just as powerful here.

"I beg you to return to life my wife Eurydice. We all must come to you some day, but please let Eurydice live a full life before she must dwell here forever."

As Orpheus sang, the ghosts began to cry. Sisyphus, who had been sentenced to forever roll a huge boulder up a steep hill—only to have it roll down again, over and over—sat against the rock to listen.

Tantalus, cursed with unquenchable thirst and gnawing hunger, heard the words and felt satisfied.

Even the hideous, cruel faces of the Furies were wet with tears.

Proserpine could not deny Orpheus's request, and Pluto called for Eurydice. She appeared from among the recently arrived spirits, limping on her wounded foot.

"You may take her back to earth on one condition," said Pluto. "She is to follow behind you, and you must not look back at her until you are both in daylight again."

Orpheus agreed.

Orpheus and Eurydice began their slow and horrifying escape from the land of the dead. Throughout, Orpheus remained a few steps ahead of his wife.

As they neared the mouth of the cave, a ray of daylight beamed in. They had nearly reached the outlet when, in a moment of forgetfulness, Orpheus turned to glance behind him. Instantly, Eurydice was whisked back into the cave's awful depths. The couple stretched out their arms for one last embrace, but clasped only the air.

"Farewell," cried Eurydice, dying a second time, "a last farewell," and she was gone.

Pygmalion

Pygmalion was a gifted sculptor who carved a life-size statue of a woman from a large piece of marble.

So beautiful was this statue that no living woman would stand near it, for fear of looking plain by comparison. It was so lifelike that it seemed about to move.

The artist truly admired his creation and at last he fell in love with it. He caressed it to remind himself that it was only stone, and he gave it presents of bright shells and polished pebbles, little birds, and colorful flowers. He had a gown designed for it, and furnished it with rings for its fingers and jewels for its neck. He brought it cushions to rest upon, as if the statue could enjoy their softness.

The festival of Venus, the love goddess, was celebrated in Pygmalion's city. Sacrifices were offered, the altars smoked, and incense thickened the air.

Pygmalion   pig-MAY-lee-un
Galatea   gal-uh-TEE-uh

Pygmalion took part in the celebration and went to the altar to pray to the goddess. Timidly he said, "Gods, you can do all things. I pray that you give me a wife like my marble maiden."

Pygmalion didn't dare say what he really wished for: he wanted his statue for a wife. But Venus knew his thoughts. As an omen of her favor, the goddess caused the ceremonial flame to shoot up into the air three times.

When Pygmalion returned home, he went to greet his statue. He kissed its mouth. It felt warm. He put his hand on its arm. It was soft and yielded to his fingers.

Afraid that he might be mistaken, he touched her again and again. She was indeed alive!

Jubilant, Pygmalion pressed his lips to lips as real as his own. The statue felt the kiss and blushed. Demurely she opened her eyes, seeing her lover for the first time. Pygmalion named the woman Galatea.

Venus blessed the couple. They lived happily together and raised a son.

Phaeton

Phaeton was the human son of the sun god Apollo. He lived on earth, and he had never met his father, who pulled the sun across the sky in his golden chariot each day. Phaeton's friends didn't believe that Phaeton was of such noble birth. Soon, he began to doubt it himself.

He said to his mother, "If I really am of heavenly birth, I need some proof."

His mother replied, "Go to India, the land where the sun rises. You'll find your father there. Ask him if he will claim you as his son."

Full of hope and pride, Phaeton went to visit his father.

The Palace of the Sun stood on huge columns, glittering with gold and precious stones. The floors were ivory and the doors were silver. On the walls were murals showing scenes of the earth, sea, and sky.

Phaeton approached Apollo. "My father, please give me some proof that I may know I'm your son."

"Son," answered Apollo, "you are indeed my own. To end your doubts, I will grant you anything you wish."

The boy immediately asked to drive the chariot of the sun across the sky.

Phaeton   FAY-uh-tun

"But Phaeton," replied the sun god, "you are human. What you ask is beyond the ability of most gods. I must keep my promise to grant your wish, but I beg you to reconsider.

"The road to the sky is steep and dangerous," Apollo warned, "and at noontime the chariot is high above the earth. To look down is terrifying. It still frightens me. The way back to earth also is very steep. All my strength is needed to slow the horses and control them.

"As for the horses themselves, they breathe fire and resist the reins.

"Do you ask me for proof that you are my son? I give you proof in my fears for you. I do not want to give you this fatal gift."

Phaeton was not persuaded by his father's speech. At last, Apollo led his son to the chariot. It was solid gold with silver spokes. Diamonds outlined the seats, reflecting the sun's brightness.

The sky began turning purple, signalling the beginning of the new day. The horses were led out of their stable. They stamped and snorted, impatient to start their journey.

Helping Phaeton into the chariot, Apollo urged, "hold the reins tightly and stay in the middle of the road. The marks of the wheels will guide you."

The horses lunged forward, surprised by the lightness of the load they carried. The chariot bumped and swayed as if empty. The terrified Phaeton tried to guide the fiery horses, but they took control and left the path.

When Phaeton looked down on the earth, he nearly fainted from fear. The horses swooped down and the boy dropped the reins. As the chariot drew closer to the earth, forests and villages burst into flame from the sun's scorching heat. The seas boiled. Oceans turned to desert. The earth was ablaze.

Then just as suddenly, the horses shot upward. The earth would have been plunged into total darkness if not for the fires that covered its face. Heat and smoke rose up, blinding Phaeton and choking him.

Jupiter, king of the gods, saw the tragedy. He tried to send rain, but all the clouds were burned away. He had but one choice.

Picking up a lightning bolt, Jupiter hurled it at the chariot. The impact jolted Phaeton out of his seat. He fell like a shooting star into the sea. The exhausted horses returned to the Palace of the Sun and to their saddened master, Apollo.

Medusa, Pegasus, and the Chimera

Medusa was once a beautiful maiden with shiny, flowing locks of hair. She dared to compare her beauty with that of Minerva, the goddess of wisdom, who changed Medusa's gorgeous ringlets into hissing serpents. Medusa became a monster so frightfully ugly that anyone who looked at her face was instantly turned to stone.

Medusa lived in a cave, surrounded by the stony figures of animals and people who had had the misfortune to catch a glimpse of her. One night, while Medusa slept, Jupiter's mortal son Perseus entered the cave and cut off her head. To avoid looking directly at Medusa, Perseus used his shield as a mirror.

Medusa	mih-DOO-suh
Pegasus	PEG-uh-sis
Chimera	kuh-MEER-uh
Perseus	PUR-see-us
Bellerophon	buh-LAIR-uh-fun

The blood from Medusa's wound created the winged horse Pegasus, who later helped to defeat another monster called the Chimera.

The Chimera was a fearsome, fire-breathing monster. The front of its body was a combination of a lion and a goat; the hind part was a dragon.

A young warrior named Bellerophon was called upon to kill the beast, even though no one believed it was possible. But Bellerophon never considered the danger.

Before going into combat with the Chimera, Bellerophon visited a prophet who told him that to succeed, he must ride Pegasus.

Bellerophon spent a restless night in the temple of Minerva, who had caught and tamed the winged steed. Minerva visited Bellerophon in a dream, gave him a golden bridle, and showed him where he could find Pegasus.

When he awoke, Bellerophon still held the bridle. Grateful that the gods had blessed him, he went to the place he had dreamed of and there he found the wonderful steed drinking from a fountain. At the sight of the bridle, Pegasus eagerly trotted over to his new master.

Bellerophon rode Pegasus to victory over the Chimera. It was the first of many victories they shared.

Arachne

There once was a talented weaver named Arachne. Her skill in the arts of weaving and embroidery was so great that the nymphs would leave their groves and fountains to watch her. She wove tapestries and cloths that were beautiful beyond belief, and the graceful way she carded and spun the rough wool into shimmering strands was thrilling to behold. Those who saw her nimble fingers work the spindle and needle had no doubt that the goddess Minerva, who invented handicrafts, had taught her.

This Arachne passionately denied. She couldn't bear to be thought of as a pupil, even of a goddess.

"Let Minerva try her skill against mine," she said. "If I lose, I will pay the penalty."

Minerva heard this and was displeased. Disguised as an old woman, she visited Arachne to give her some advice:

"I have had much experience," said she, "and I hope you will let me speak. Challenge any mortal you wish, but do not compete with a goddess.

"I advise you also to ask Minerva's forgiveness," she added. "Because she is merciful, perhaps she will pardon you."

Arachne stopped spinning and replied, "Old woman, save your advice for your daughters or handmaids. I stand by what I say.

"I am not afraid of the goddess; let her try her skill, if she dare."

At this, Minerva dropped her disguise. The nymphs bowed low in respect.

"So let us begin, then," said the goddess.

Arachne blushed, then grew pale, but she confidently threaded her loom.

Arachne   uh-RAK-nee
Minerva   mih-NUR-vuh

The goddess and Arachne worked quickly in the excitement of the contest. Both blended the colors of their threads as delicately as the stripes of a rainbow blend invisibly from one color to the next.

Minerva's cloth depicted the gods. In the corners she wove pictures showing the gods' displeasure with humans who dared to challenge them.

For her cloth, Arachne chose subjects showing the failings and errors of the gods. Her weaving was wonderfully well done. Minerva couldn't help but admire Arachne's work, but could not forgive the insult. She tore Arachne's cloth and then touched the mortal's forehead, making Arachne feel her own guilt. Deeply ashamed, Arachne made a noose to hang herself.

But Minerva pitied Arachne as she saw her hanging from
the rope.

"Live, guilty woman!" she exclaimed. "So that you will not
forget this lesson, may you and your descendants continue to hang
for all time."

Minerva touched Arachne once again. Immediately Arachne's
hair fell away, as did her nose and ears. Her head grew smaller and
her body shrank. Her fingers clung to her side and became legs. In
this way, Minerva transformed Arachne into a spider.

Even today, the spider spins webs that none can duplicate.
Scientists call spiders and their relatives arachnids to honor this
once-proud maiden.

Cupid and Psyche

Beauty was a curse to a young woman named Psyche. She was so lovely that people traveled great distances just to look at her.

Venus, the goddess of love, was jealous of Psyche's beauty and the attention she received from her admirers. She often complained to her son, Cupid, about it. Cupid was a mischievous young god with golden curls and white wings. It was his job to cause men and women to fall in love by shooting them with his magic arrows.

Venus one day told her son, "My boy, Psyche's beauty gives me great pain. My temples are empty because men flock to her. Punish her and give your mother a sweet revenge. Make her fall in love with some unworthy soul so that she may embarrass herself and disgrace her family."

To carry out this plan, Cupid visited Psyche while she slept. Psyche was so beautiful that Cupid felt a twinge of pity for her. He sprinkled bitter water on her lips to spoil her future happiness, and then he pricked her with his arrow to make her fall in love.

At the touch of the arrow, Psyche awoke and looked directly at Cupid. The impish god was invisible, but he was startled. In his confusion, Cupid accidentally jabbed himself with his own arrow without realizing it.

His compassion for Psyche grew, and he sprinkled sweet water upon her hair to undo his spell. He had fallen completely in love with her.

Psyche	SY-kee
Ceres	SER-eez
Proserpine	PRAHS-ur-pyn

Cupid's wound was tended by Venus, who hated Psyche more than ever. Venus made sure that even though Psyche remained popular, no man would ask for her hand.

Tired of her beauty and saddened by her solitude, Psyche began to believe she would never be married. Her parents thought she might have somehow angered the gods. They asked the advice of a prophet, who said:

"Psyche will be the bride of no mortal lover. Her future husband awaits her on the top of the mountain. He is a monster whom neither gods nor men can resist."

Her parents were horrified, but Psyche said to them:

"This is my fate for being compared to Venus. Lead me to the mountain where my miserable destiny awaits."

Psyche was brought to the mountain, panting with fear, her eyes full of tears. Suddenly a breeze lifted her up and brought her to a flowery meadow in front of a magnificent palace.

Hesitantly, she entered. Inside the palace was everything she could have wished for. She saw no one, but a voice addressed her, saying:

"Good lady, we whose voices you hear are your servants, and we shall obey your commands with the utmost care."

Psyche went to her chamber to rest. When she wanted dinner, she saw the table magically set without the aid of any servant.

The palace was the home of Cupid. He came to visit her each night and was always gone by morning. Psyche never saw his face or knew his name, but he was gentle and caring. Psyche soon grew to love him and began to think of him as her husband. She often begged him to stay and let her see him, but he always refused.

"Why should you wish to behold me?" Cupid asked. "Have you any doubt of my love? Have you any wish ungratified?

"If you saw me, perhaps you would fear me, perhaps adore me," Cupid continued, "but all I ask is to love me."

This satisfied Psyche for a while. Then she began to think about her family, who didn't know her fate. One night, she asked Cupid to send for her two sisters so they could see that all was well.

Psyche's sisters came and saw Psyche's splendid home. They asked what her husband was like, and she had to admit that she'd never seen him.

"Remember," warned one of the sisters, "the prophet said you would marry a monster. People who live in this valley say your husband is a serpent who will fatten you up and then devour you."

"Take our advice," said her other sister; "keep a lamp and a sharp knife near your bed. When your husband is sound asleep, light the lamp and look at him. If he is a monster, cut off his head."

At first Psyche rejected her sisters' advice, but soon their words and her own curiosity were too strong to resist.

One night, as Cupid lay sleeping, Psyche lit the lamp and held it to her husband's face. What she saw was not a hideous monster, but the most beautiful of the gods, with golden ringlets wandering over his pale neck, and with two magnificent wings, white as snow, on his shoulders.

As Psyche leaned forward to get a closer look, a few drops of burning oil from the lamp fell on one shoulder of the god. He opened his eyes and, without saying a word, flew out the window. Psyche ran out of the house to follow him, but she stumbled and fell in the dust.

Cupid, turning to look at her, said, "Foolish Psyche, is this how you repay my love? Return to your sisters, whose advice you think is better than mine. I punish you by leaving you forever. Love cannot dwell with suspicion."

Cupid flew off, and the house and gardens vanished with him.

Psyche did not return to her parents' home. Instead she wandered the land, searching for Cupid. One morning, she spied a magnificent temple upon a lofty mountain. "Perhaps my love lives there," she thought, and rushed toward it.

Inside she found a jumble of corn, barley, wheat, and a variety of farm tools. Psyche went to work straightening up the temple, believing that she shouldn't neglect any of the gods. The temple belonged to Ceres, the goddess of the harvest. Pleased by Psyche's work, Ceres said:

"Psyche, you are truly worthy of my help. Though I can't protect you from Venus, I can tell you how to win her favor. It is she who is keeping your husband from you. Seek Venus and modestly ask her forgiveness. Perhaps then you and Cupid shall be reunited."

Psyche went to the temple of Venus and prayed to the goddess. The goddess appeared and led Psyche to a huge pigeon coop, which contained piles of assorted beans and seeds.

Venus told Psyche that she must separate all of the grains by evening. Psyche, knowing the task was impossible, sat and wept. But Cupid was watching. He ordered the ants to separate the pile grain by grain. By twilight the job was done.

When Venus returned, she was furious.

"This was no work of yours, wicked one!" shouted the goddess of love. "I have another task for you."

The next morning, Venus led Psyche to a river. Across the river was an enormous flock of sheep with golden wool. Psyche was told to collect a bit of golden fleece from each sheep.

Psyche went to the riverside to follow the order. But the river god said, "Oh maiden, do not try to cross this raging river nor approach the sheep on the other side. The river is at its roughest now, and the rams are at their wildest. Wait until noon; then you may cross the water safely, and you will find the woolly gold sticking to the bushes and trunks of the trees.

Her task accomplished, Psyche returned to Venus with her arms full of the golden fleece.

"I know very well that you could not have done this task by yourself," said Venus. "But I have another task, one that you must do on your own."

"Take this box," ordered Venus, "and give it to Proserpine, the queen of the underworld. Tell her that I have sent you to collect a little of her beauty, for I have lost mine through worrying about my son."

Psyche was certain that this was to be the end of her. Few mortals had ever entered the land of the dead and then returned. She climbed a high cliff and prepared to jump, thinking this was the fastest way to the underworld, when a voice said:

"Poor unlucky girl, what cowardice you are showing! Why do you think the gods who have helped you thus far would abandon you now?"

The voice told Psyche of a safe passage to the underworld, and warned:

"When Proserpine has given you the box filled with her beauty, you must never open it."

Psyche did as she was told. When she was back among the living, she thought it would please her husband if she put a little of Proserpine's divine beauty on her own cheeks. She opened the box. It contained not beauty but deep sleep. Psyche fell to the ground, overcome by drowsiness.

Cupid, seeing what had happened, flew to the spot where Psyche lay, drew the sleep from her body, and put it back in the box. "Again," said he, "you have almost perished by your curiosity. But still I love you."

Cupid then flew to Olympus, where the gods lived, and presented himself to Jupiter, the ruler of the gods. He told Jupiter of his undying love for Psyche and asked him to help persuade his mother that Psyche would be a worthy wife. Jupiter agreed to help, and Venus consented to the marriage.

Psyche was brought before all the gods and was handed a cup of ambrosia, the food of the gods.

"Drink this, Psyche," said Jupiter, "and become immortal." In this way, Psyche became a goddess, and she and Cupid were united forever.

Atalanta

In the ancient world, where men were brave and heroic, and women delicate and beautiful, there lived Atalanta, a woman who had both beauty and strength.

Atalanta was raised by a clan of bears who taught her to hunt and defend herself. She grew to be a natural athlete, whose long, slender legs could carry her swiftly and quietly through her forest home. She could spring like a panther, outrun a deer. To build her strength, she playfully wrestled her childhood friends, the bears. She also taught herself archery and became a first-class shot.

But soon Atalanta yearned to join her own people. The proper Greek women would have nothing to do with her—how could they accept a woman who wrestled bears for fun? What could they say to a woman who felt no need for makeup or fine gowns or jewelry? They could never accept Atalanta—but the truth was that Atalanta wasn't very fond of them, either. She had more in common with the Greek men.

At first the men objected when Atalanta joined their tournaments and hunts, but it was soon obvious to everyone that her skills were almost godlike. Atalanta earned the men's respect and they let her participate.

Calydonian	KAL-ih-DO-nee-in
Meleager	mel-ee-AY-jur
Hippomenes	hih-POM-uh-neez

Atalanta's most famous adventure was the hunt for the Calydonian Boar. This wild beast of enormous size was destroying the countryside. Its eyes shone with blood and fire, its bristles stood out like spears, and its tusks were like those of an Indian elephant.

Meleager, the prince of Calydon, summoned all the heroes of Greece to help destroy this monster. With them came Atalanta. A buckle of polished gold clasped her vest, an ivory quiver hung from her left shoulder, and her left hand bore her bow. As soon as he saw her, Meleager loved her. Atalanta felt the same stirrings for him. Together they killed the boar.

Their happiness was not meant to be. The Destinies, three dreaded sisters who weave, measure, and cut the thread of life, decided that Meleager's life would be short. Soon after the great hunt, he was dead.

Having lost the man she loved, Atalanta fled from society and devoted herself to hunting and running. But she was not so easily forgotten. Many suitors sought her hand. She impatiently refused them. To regain her privacy, Atalanta made this condition:

"I will marry the man who shall conquer me in a footrace; but death must be the penalty of all who lose."

Many suitors felt it was worth the risk. Each raced Atalanta, and each was quickly killed.

Hippomenes, a witness to the contest, loved Atalanta and accepted her challenge. Atalanta, who was equally fond of Hippomenes, hoped he would not be foolish enough to race her. "What god can tempt one so young to throw himself away?" she asked herself as they waited for the signal.

But Hippomenes had a plan. He prayed to Venus, the goddess of love, who gave him three golden apples, which he hid beneath his robe.

At the signal, Atalanta and Hippomenes skimmed down the track, shoulder to shoulder. The cries of the spectators cheered Hippomenes, but his breath began to fail him, his throat was dry, and the goal was still far away. At that moment he threw down one of the golden apples. Amazed, Atalanta stopped to pick it up.

Hippomenes shot ahead. Shouts burst forth from all sides.

Atalanta began to close the gap. Again Hippomenes dropped an apple. Atalanta paused to scoop it up, but then drew still closer. The goal was near; one chance remained for Hippomenes.

"Now, goddess," he said, "do not fail me!" and threw the last apple to one side. Atalanta saw it fall and hesitated—but Venus made the apple irresistible. Atalanta chased the apple and lost the race.

And so the two lovers were married.

Baucis and Philemon

The gods were often devilish, but they could also be compassionate.

Baucis and her husband Philemon were an elderly mortal couple who shared their quiet lives in a simple, thatched hut. One night, two weary travelers knocked on their door. Philemon welcomed them while Baucis, bustling and attentive, spread a cloth and bid them to sit.

They had very little to offer the strangers, but Baucis and Philemon were free with what they did have. As Baucis kindled a fire, Philemon prepared some herbs and bacon for a stew and poured some wine from an earthenware pitcher.

Baucis, with her apron on and her old hands trembling, set the table. One table leg was shorter than the rest, but a piece of slate set it right. The strangers were given cushions to sit on, and the four enjoyed their modest meal and each other's friendly company.

As the meal proceeded, the old couple were astonished to see that the pitcher of wine refilled itself as fast as it was poured. Struck with terror, Baucis and Philemon realized their guests were gods. Falling upon their knees, they begged forgiveness for their humble hospitality. To honor the gods, they offered to make a sacrifice of an old goose that they kept as guardian of their hut, but the bird was too nimble and scurried about, avoiding capture.

Baucis   BAH-sis
Philemon   fih-LEE-mon

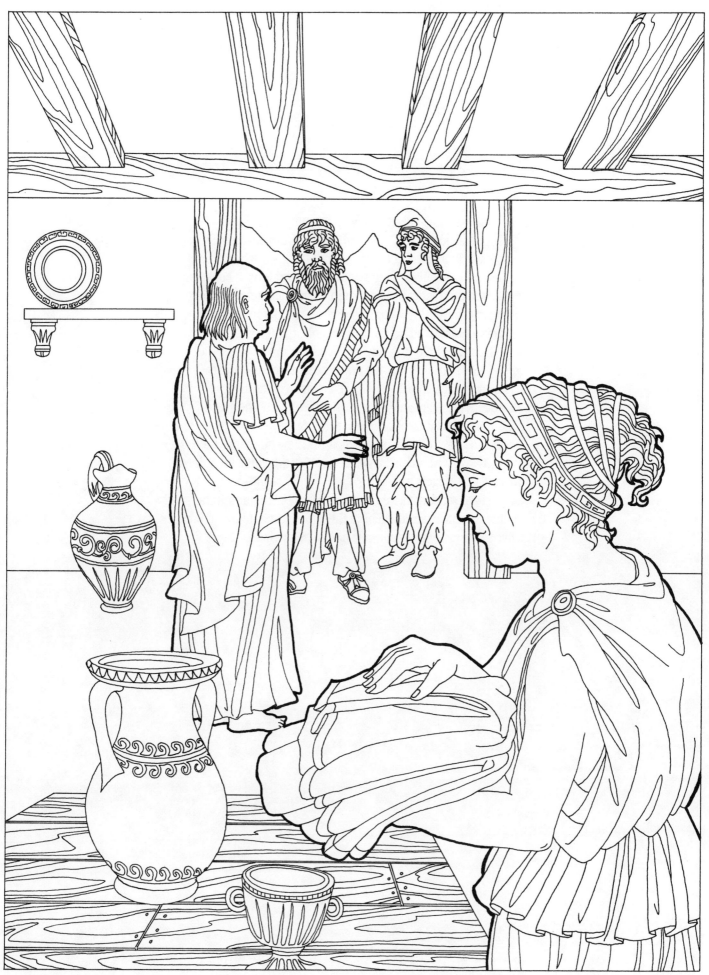

The two gods forbade the slaughter of the goose. They revealed themselves to be Jupiter and his son, Mercury, and they told the couple:

"This inhospitable village shall pay the penalty for its disrespect; you alone shall be saved. Come with us to the top of yonder hill."

Baucis and Philemon, accompanied by the gods, labored up the steep incline. When they were near the top, they looked back and saw their village sunken in a lake, with only their own house left standing.

As they lamented the fate of their neighbors, their old house was changed into a temple: columns replaced the corner posts, the thatched roof became gold, the floors became marble, and the doors were enriched with carving and ornamentation.

"Excellent old man, and woman worthy of such a husband," spoke Jupiter, "what favor have you to ask of us?"

Philemon spoke quietly with Baucis for a few moments, then answered, "We wish to be the guardians of your temple for as long as we may live.

"Also, since we have passed our lives in love with one another, we wish that when we die, it will be at the same moment, so that I may not live to see my wife's grave, nor be lain in my own by her."

Their prayer was granted and they lived for many years as keepers of the temple.

As they stood one day at the steps of the great building, Baucis saw Philemon begin to put forth leaves, while Philemon saw Baucis changing as well. Soon a leafy crown grew over their heads.

"Farewell dear spouse," they said together, and at the same moment bark closed over their mouths. They had become two trees whose intertwining branches were a living monument to their lifelong love.